MAKERSPACES™

GETTING THE MOST OUT OF
MAKERSPACES
TO MAKE
MUSICAL INSTRUMENTS

GREG ROZA

ROSEN
PUBLISHING®

New York

Published in 2015 by The Rosen Publishing Group, Inc.
29 East 21st Street, New York, NY 10010

Copyright © 2015 by The Rosen Publishing Group, Inc.

First Edition

Library of Congress Cataloging-in-Publication Data

Roza, Greg, author.
Getting the most out of makerspaces to make musical instruments/Greg Roza.—First edition.
      pages cm.—(makerspaces)
Audience: Grades 5–8.
Includes bibliographical references and index.
ISBN 978-1-4777-7823-4 (library bound)—ISBN 978-1-4777-7825-8 (pbk.)—ISBN 978-1-4777-7826-5 (6-pack)
1. Musical instruments—Construction—Juvenile literature. 2. Do-it-yourself work—Juvenile literature. I. Title.
ML460.R69 2015
784.192—dc23

2013051218

Manufactured in the United States of America.

CONTENTS

INTROD

Attendees of a recent World Maker Faire in New York City participate in a group activity.

Most people like music, and many people like to make music. But not everyone has the means to pursue musical training. New instruments are expensive, as are supplies and private lessons. Although many people buy used instruments, they can be costly, too.

As many do-it-yourselfers out there will say, there's always a way to pursue musical training, including through personal exploration. For centuries, people have been making instruments from items they've found in nature. People still follow ancient traditions and practices for making instruments. Thanks to modern innovations—such as plastics, electrical equipment, and new musical styles—musicians have limitless tools and supplies to choose from. You can find this and a lot more when you visit a makerspace where musicians meet to experiment, share, learn, and teach.

The term "makerspace" refers specifically to the physical location where a do-it-yourself movement (called the maker movement) is cultivated. This could be a library, a school, a warehouse, or even a basement. Makerspaces are a relatively new phenomenon, but they have really taken off as more and more people discover them. They provide an environment that is both fun and educational. Makerspaces make learning easier because they are all about sharing—that includes knowledge, time, supplies, tools, and, of course, workspaces.

What goes on at a music-themed makerspace? Many offer classes on how to build simple traditional instruments, such as drums and flutes. Some makerspaces may have a central focus, such as drum making, electronic music, and music software. Others, such as the extensive guitar-making groups in the country, are highly specialized. Many music makerspaces are taking advantage of modern methods and techniques to help spread knowledge to others.

Many makerspaces don't have a central theme. Rather, they provide a rich environment where people get together and learn from each other. Makerspaces allow you to hang out with friends and meet people who have similar interests. They are community meeting places where individuals can immerse themselves in technical and musical environments. They also help people pursue their goals, regardless of their financial situation.

The people you'll meet at makerspaces are often neighborly and enthusiastic. Some are there to learn new things, but many are there to teach. You will find men, women, adults, and young people, but also craftspeople, carpenters, electricians, engineers, musicians, writers, and many others. Some are hobbyists and some are professionals, but they are all "makers."

This variety of people and talents creates the perfect environment for communal learning while providing an outlet for creative ingenuity. Feedback from peers is one of the best ways to fine-tune your skills and talent. In time, you may get fulfillment from helping others improve as well.

Once you give it a try, you'll find that it's not so hard to make basic instruments, and you will learn a lot as you go. But that's just the beginning. Music makerspaces are a fun way to learn more about countless instruments, as well as musical styles, performances, innovations, and much more.

CHAPTER ONE

WHAT'S IT ALL ABOUT?

Makerspaces are based on the idea of knowing how to do things for yourself, rather than relying on someone else. Do it yourself (DIY) is a frame of mind and a lifestyle for some people, such as those who are into home improvement. They get enormous fulfillment from being able to fix a sink, build a deck, install new lights, and many other money-saving home improvement projects. Home improvement is just one example. There are makerspaces out there for just about any theme you can think of, including music.

Musicians are creative people who enjoy learning new things and sharing the experience with others. Most enjoy performing with other musicians. You can find other musicians to jam with at music makerspaces, but you can also learn to make instruments, fix instruments, and experience the latest trends and innovations.

JUST DO IT

Perhaps the most effective way to learn something is to simply do it. That's exactly how many great musicians learned to play music. Rock musician Jimi Hendrix is often considered the greatest guitarist ever, and he was completely self-taught. Not every musician is a Jimi Hendrix, but many have the same drive to learn and play. If you enjoy playing music, keep going. Other musicians you meet at makerspaces can help you improve as well.

Innovative musicians are not always happy to play factory instruments, so they modify and rebuild store-bought instruments. Others love to build their own from scratch. When he was young, rock pioneer Bo Diddley built his own violin and upright bass before creating his signature rectangular electric guitar. What could be more fulfilling for a musician than to make the very instrument he or she makes music with? The right makerspace can provide you with an opportunity to watch experienced instrument makers at work. You can learn their skills, try them out, get valuable feedback, and have fun all the while.

SHARING THE WEALTH

Sharing knowledge, ideas, tools, and supplies allows everyone to benefit in some way. Makerspaces are often funded by private sources, so there are numerous ways for an individual to help make them successful. Many makerspaces require members to pay dues. This money may go to space rental, utility bills, supplies, and other costs.

Junk shops are the perfect place to find old instruments to turn into projects. You may find some at garage sales, too.

Makerspaces need tools and supplies, but they can't always afford them. Some members donate extra supplies or allow others to use their tools. They may even find materials in thrift shops, junkyards, and dumpsters. Someone might be able to teach you how to repair that broken bass guitar in your basement.

9

MAKERS RECYCLE

Have you ever thrown out a toy, instrument, or computer just because it was no longer functioning, or "dead"? Even though a machine may not be worth fixing, many are loaded with valuable parts that makerspaces thrive on. By recycling, makerspaces collect valuable supplies and save money.

You may not need that old fan anymore, but a makerspace could use the metal parts, plastic parts, electrical wires, circuitry, and motor. They would even take the knobs or buttons if the fan has them. A fan motor that has been repaired and cleaned up might be used to make a remote-controlled car or maybe even a music box. Even the smallest nuts and bolts have value. This economy of resources helps many makerspaces to stay open.

Taking machines apart is a great learning experience. Have you ever wondered how a guitar amplifier works? Taking a broken one apart can help you understand how they function and maybe even how to make your own. You can also salvage parts for later. (Never dismantle anything without permission from and the help of an adult. It can be dangerous to dismantle electronics and machines with moving parts.)

Sharing tools and supplies is just the beginning. Musical makerspaces are the perfect place to share knowledge. People meet to discuss and experiment with music and other technologies. There are opportunities to meet musicians to jam with or even to form a band. Others provide a fun environment where you can learn the basics about making instruments. Regardless of the focus, all makerspaces are intended to foster learning through participation, involvement, and sharing.

BUILDING A NETWORK

The people you know form a web of interactions. The more people you know, the larger your web becomes. This is called a network. Interacting with the people in your network helps build valuable connections with others who might be able to help you in the future.

Many people in your network are very close to you: mom, dad, siblings, and friends. Others are acquaintances, such as coaches, teachers, or neighbors. As part of your network, you might mow a neighbor's lawn, and he might help rake your leaves. Having a network means that you have dependable people to lean on when you need them.

A professional network is made up of the friends and acquaintances who can help you excel in a career. Let's say you learned how to string a guitar online and you share the information with a friend. In turn, your friend may help you repair a snare drum head or teach you how to use music-related

11

software. It's this kind of back-and-forth interaction that helps foster a network with reliable contacts. It's also similar to the way a makerspace works, where the participants are interested in forming lasting relationships that are beneficial for everyone.

FINDING A MENTOR

Is there someone in your life who took the time to teach you something new? Chances are you can think of several people: relatives, friends, teachers, coaches. These people are mentors. They are often older than you, but that's not always the case. Mentors are more experienced, and they help foster learning in less experienced people.

Joining a makerspace is a good way to find a mentor. Not everyone you meet there will prove to be a mentor, but many are drawn to helping others learn and improve. A makerspace itself can serve as a mentor of sorts. It can both help motivate and inspire young minds.

CHAPTER TWO

THE SHORT HISTORY OF MAKERSPACES

People have gathered to discuss music, experiment with musical styles, and make new musical instruments for thousands of years. Native American groups made many kinds of instruments with the materials available to them. These included simple rock or wood percussion instruments, but they also used more creative techniques, such as crafting flutes from clay and using animal bladders for drum heads. Music was deeply connected to their beliefs and ways of life, and instrument-making traditions were passed down over the generations. Today, some people still use Native American methods to make similar instruments.

We now have far more techniques and materials to choose from. You can work with traditional materials, or you can use the latest high-tech tools. Makerspaces help make this possible. It's hard to say exactly when makerspaces originated, but they have always had the same mission: to bring people together and share knowledge.

13

HACKERS AND MAKERS

The first makerspaces were called hackerspaces. They were formed by computer programmers, or "hackers," for the purpose of founding a headquarters where they could meet to discuss, experiment with, and share ideas about programming.

This annual gathering of hackers at the Chaos Computer Club took place in Berlin, Germany.

One of the first known hackerspaces is called c-base. It opened its doors in Berlin, Germany, in 1995, and it's still open today. It has become known as a mecca for hackers who advocate digital freedom on the Internet and criticize government regulations. It wasn't until 2007 that a group of American hackers visited c-base and other European hackerspaces, which helped start a similar movement in the United States.

The term "hacker" began taking on a new meaning. In many circles today "hack" is synonymous with "do it yourself." As people began founding hackerspaces that catered to interests other than programming, a new term emerged: makerspace. Some people feel there's no difference between the two terms. Others feel "makerspace" describes places that feature a wider range of interests—from home improvement to musical instruments.

"Makerspace" and "hackerspace" are general terms that arose out of the do-it-yourself movement. Before "makerspace" became a widely used term, several groups established community-based learning centers with all the tools and technologies necessary to create numerous products, from start to finish. They helped give momentum to the DIY movement in the United States. Two of the most notable groups are FabLabs and Tech Shops. Both were initiated by universities, and they continue to bring makers together.

GO TO THE FAIRE

In 2006, *Make* magazine held the first Maker Faire in San Mateo, California. More than twenty thousand people attended

This recent Maker Faire in Rome, Italy, was a huge success. About thirty-five thousand people attended the faire.

the two-day event to see hundreds of "show-and-tell" projects made by do-it-yourselfers of all ages. The event was such a success that it started an increasingly popular Maker Faire movement. These gatherings allow makers to show their inventions to the public and share the knowledge that they've learned with others. It's also a chance for people to experience new technologies and new uses for old technologies up close.

Recently, 165,000 people attended two Maker Faires held in California and New York. However, Maker Faires have also inspired communities all over the country and around the world to hold Mini Maker Faires (in what some are calling the Maker Faire movement). These are similar to the regular events, but they take place in local libraries, schools, and parks, and they feature the work of local makers. While these events often focus on high-tech inventions, they are also closely tied to artistic and musical creations. People who attended a recent Mini Maker Faire in Santiago, Chile, were treated to live music played on instruments made from recycled materials. It's this kind of musical ingenuity that keeps music lovers going back for more. Others are inspired to attend the next event or even start their own makerspace.

INTO THE FUTURE

Makerspaces and hackerspaces are physical places where people can work together on a myriad of fun and useful projects. While some makerspaces focus on a specific type of technology, many have transformed into all-purpose community resource centers that cater to numerous tastes and interests. While they were once difficult to find, Makerspaces have grown and spread across the country. They are helping transform schools and libraries into technical training grounds for young scientists, programmers, craftspeople, and musicians. They have also allowed a wider range of people to have access to makerspaces.

Makerspaces sometimes offer a classroom type of setting in order to teach larger groups a concept.

JUG BAND INSTRUMENTS

Makerspaces might be a new movement, but DIY musicians have been making instruments for a long time. Jug bands from the early 1900s are a perfect example. At this time, jazz and the blues were gaining attention, and many musicians made a living playing on steamboats and in river cities. Not everyone could afford to buy new instruments, so they often made their own from the materials available to them. The whiskey jug, for example, was used in place of tubas and other low-range instruments. This is where the term "jug band" comes from. Jug bands played in many locations along the Mississippi and Ohio Rivers. They reached the height of their popularity in the 1920s and 1930s.

Poor jug band musicians found many ways to improvise. Some attached an old guitar neck to a hollowed-out gourd to create a whole new instrument. Other common jug band instruments include the washboard, spoons, washtub bass, and comb-and-paper kazoo. The money-saving ideas that led to jug bands influenced future generations of DIY musicians. These are instruments that people still make and use today.

The Internet and makerspaces have helped keep jug band instruments in the spotlight. Many of the instruments are easy to make and play, and they make great DIY projects. Each year, jug band festivals bring instrument makers, musicians, and music fans together. This includes the annual Battle of the Jug Bands in Minneapolis, Minnesota, which has been held since 1980.

CHAPTER THREE

A TOUR OF MAKERSPACES

Makerspaces are fun places to explore. It's like walking into a science fair, college laboratory, and tech shop, all rolled into one unique place. As a musician or instrument maker, what can you expect to get out of a local makerspace? Let's see what makerspaces have to offer.

A SPACE FOR MAKERS

As previously mentioned, without the physical places where makerspaces function, there would be no makerspaces. But not every makerspace is going to look the same. Some are set up for a specific focus, such as metalworking, 3-D printing, or electronic music. Every makerspace has its own look and feel, but many offer the same basic features.

The size of makerspaces ranges from cramped garages to spacious warehouses. It depends on the location, funding, and type of makerspace. You may find small rented spaces in schools, colleges, and libraries. They might be small, but they often have the tools, supplies, and leadership necessary to be successful. Larger spaces offer plenty of room with stations where numerous activities can take place at the same time.

INNER SPACE

Most makerspaces feature several basic workstations, compartments, or labs. Electronics play an important role in many makerspaces, so most have an electronics workbench and a soldering station. A power tool area features numerous tools and benches for projects, as well as protective gear. Some have a large area where multiple projects can take shape. Computer stations provide a workspace for programmers, designers, electronic musicians, and many others. Laser engraving and 3-D printing have become very popular, and they are becoming commonplace in most makerspaces. Other stations may include sound studios, vinyl cutting areas, sewing areas, painting and sculpting stations, welding shops, greens screens, and more.

Makerspaces aren't always set up specifically for musicians and instrument makers. However, musicians often take advantage of the tools found in them. A makerspace woodshop might have everything you need to make your own wooden guitar. Metalworking tools can be used to make wind and percussion instruments. If you're into electronic music, you're in luck: most makerspaces feature electronics labs and digital music stations. Makerspaces aim to appeal to as many people as possible in an attempt to foster a hands-on approach to learning valuable skills.

Learning to solder—with adult supervision, of course—is an important skill when working with electronics. It's one of the first things you'll learn at a makerspace.

ESSENTIAL SUPPLIES

Finding supplies can be a makerspace's greatest hurdle. Not only do they require up-to-date tools and computers, but they also need a steady flow of materials for projects. As an instrument maker, think of all the supplies you may need: wood, metal, electrical wiring, paints, and more. Makerspaces need to fund these supplies, and they can be expensive. This shows why makerspaces thrive on recycling, sharing, and donating.

A well-stocked makerspace can have a wide variety of materials. These include small things such as nails, screws, nuts, and bolts. Lumber, plywood, and sheet metal are some of the larger materials. Many instrument makers have discovered the value of PVC pipes. Other resources may include electrical parts, sewing material, paints, sandpaper, and so much more. And don't forget that like any public space, makerspaces need paper towels, garbage bags, brooms, and other everyday necessities. Makerspaces search for ways to keep stations well stocked, but it isn't always easy. It's good that makers are usually very resourceful.

PAYING THE RENT

The people who establish a makerspace, whether an enterprising do-it-yourselfer or the employees of a city library, need to pay bills to keep the service open to the public. Makerspaces are, at the core, physical places where people meet. Those locations usually need to be paid for. Beyond that, there are supplies, tools, and perhaps the occasional guest instructor.

The more specific the projects become at a makerspace, the greater the budget is likely to be. When you are sponsoring a program on, say, bamboo flutes, you may need to raise the funds to purchase bamboo and tools for people to use. If a makerspace has a power tool station, it's going to need proper electrical wiring. These are just a few of the reasons that makerspaces need volunteers and contributions to stay open.

PVC PIPES AND PAN FLUTES

You might think making an instrument from spare parts is hard, but creative makers know how to make use of the supplies they have. Many musicians have found new ways to use old instruments. Others have used new materials to create traditional instruments.

PVC pipes are made for construction projects, but they have been used for many other purposes, including musical instruments. Making a PVC pan flute is a great project for a new maker. Traditionally, pan flutes are made of wood. Much like a pipe organ, the pan flute's pipes are cut to specific lengths so they make specific notes when a musician blows over their open ends. Craftspeople and musicians still enjoy making and playing pan flutes. Many online resources offer instructions on how to make PVC pan flutes.

One of the most unique PVC instruments often goes by the name PVC pipe instrument. Young inventor and musician Kent Jenkins built an elaborate PVC pipe instrument that he calls the RimbaTubes. Jenkins was inspired to make the instrument after seeing the Blue Man Group play a similar instrument during a show. His version uses about 120 feet (36 meters) of PVC pipe. The ends of thirty-two pipes face upward and then wind together artistically until they are facing the audience. Jenkins makes his own paddle-like mallets to strike the tops of the pipes, creating booming notes. Each tube is "tuned" and creates a series of notes similar to a piano. Jenkins's invention became an Internet sensation when a video of him playing it appeared online.

The RimbaTubes are a complex undertaking, especially for a new maker.

Making a pan flute will help familiarize you with PVC pipes as well as some key power tools.

However, detailed instructions can be found online. You don't have to be as ambitious with your instrument designs as Kent Jenkins, but his ingenuity shows what can be achieved with the supplies you have on hand.

CHAPTER FOUR

PLAYING WITH MUSICAL TRADITIONS

In 1977, writer and musician Dallas Cline released the book *How to Play Nearly Everything*. Cline's book explains how to make numerous working instruments from everyday objects. These include traditional jug band instruments but also crazy projects such as the nose flute. Cline's book influenced and inspired a new generation of musicians to create their own instruments from everyday supplies that they might have lying around the house.

As a new instrument maker, you are in luck. Thanks to centuries of experiments with music and materials found in the natural world, there are literally thousands of instruments you can make. The real challenge is using old materials and methods in new and innovative ways.

A LONG, MUSICAL HISTORY

Recently, archaeologists in Germany found ivory flutes that are forty-two thousand to forty-three thousand

Instrument maker and musician Ken Butler rocks out on a shovel guitar that he built during a recent World Maker Faire in New York City.

years old. This shows how long people have been using materials from their surroundings to make instruments. Other ancient instruments include bone pipes and wooden drums.

You probably won't find too many people making bone flutes anymore, but this shows you that making instruments is intertwined with human evolution. With a little bit of instruction, you can start making your own simple instruments from traditional supplies and techniques in very little time. Once you've become familiar with basic instruments, you may move on to more complicated instruments, such as stringed instruments and instruments with moving parts. Using traditional supplies doesn't mean that you need to use traditional methods. It can be both fun and fulfilling to find new ways to use traditional supplies.

AN INTERVIEW WITH MAKER MUSICIAN KEN BUTLER

Ken Butler is a musician and artist who specializes in making stringed instruments out of everyday objects. He's been creating instruments for over thirty years. Some of his "hybrid instruments" are truly amazing. Butler's artwork has appeared in museums all over the world, and he has performed with numerous professional musicians.

Q: How old were you when you started playing music?

A: I started playing the viola in seventh grade in Portland, Oregon. Most people wanted to play violin, but I selected the viola and said, "I like the sound of that fat violin."

Q: Tell us about the first instrument you ever made. How many instruments have you made since that one?

A: I created my first hybrid instrument quite by accident in 1978, by adding a fingerboard, tailpiece, tuning pegs, and bridge to a small hatchet. I then played the hatchet as a violin, amplified by a small contact microphone. Since then, I have created over four hundred hybrid instruments.

Q: What is the weirdest thing you've ever used to make an instrument?

A: Hard to say, as there are so many, but perhaps my umbrella violin.

Q: What advice would you have for kids who want to make their own instruments?

A: If you're working with a string instrument, make sure that the "body" of the instrument is very strong and stiff so it can hold the tension when the string is attached and tightened. Be creative; think outside the box. Any object can be turned into a musical instrument with some creativity.

Q: What do you like most about making your own instruments?

A: It's exciting to imagine what something might sound like when you first visualize the instrument. It's a motivating force that can drive you toward the final moment when the strings are added and tuned up, finally revealing the sound.

WIND PIPES FOR EDINBURGH

Pipe organs are found mainly in old churches, and not many people get to play them. Sarah Kenchington is a musician from Glasgow, Scotland. She wanted to make a pipe organ accessible to anyone who wants to try playing one. She gathered old organ pipes from junk shops, junkyards, and online marketplaces. With more than one hundred recycled organ pipes, Wind Pipes for Edinburgh is Kenchington's largest creation. Levers with buttons made out of two-pence coins allow people to play the pipe organ. Each pipe is wrapped with brightly colored string to help people know which levers to push to play a song. To generate enough air to play the giant instrument, six people are needed to keep bellows pumping air into the machine. It's truly a community instrument.

You don't have to be a trained musician to play the Wind Pipes for Edinburgh—you just have to love music. Kenchington has made the instrument available to anyone who wants to play it.

Sarah Kenchington demonstrates how to play a much smaller version of the Wind Pipes for Edinburgh. Notice she's sitting on the bellows to keep air flowing into the instrument.

CHAPTER FIVE

GOING HI-TECH

Makerspaces have their roots in state-of-the-art advances, especially those involving computer programing and electronics. This makes them the perfect places to experiment with new technologies. Modern developments in science and computers have given artists and musicians far more options when creating instruments.

Music is closely related to math and science in many ways. If you enjoy scientific subjects, you might love creating music with some of the newest technologies found in makerspaces. Chances are that you'll find many of the modern tools mentioned in this chapter when you walk into one.

ELECTRICITY BASICS

How much do you know about electricity, electronics, and circuitry? What do you know about computer programming? How about the science of sound? Having at least a basic understanding of topics like these can help you grow as a musician but also as a maker. Safety is key when working with electricity, power tools, and heavy equipment. You may need to learn these basics before creating the latest in high-tech instruments. Fortunately, others who attend makerspaces will show you the ropes and keep you safe.

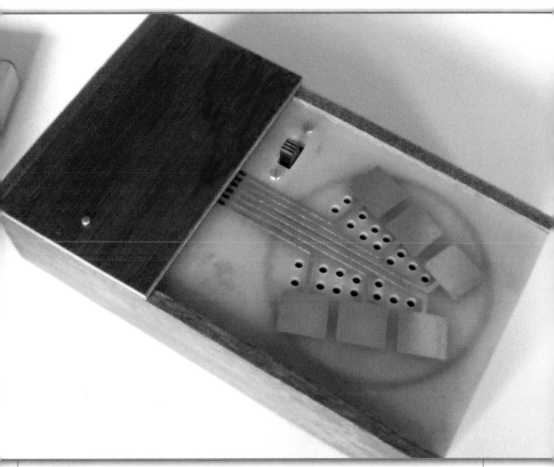

A Kraakdoos, or Cracklebox, is a noise-making electronic machine. It can be made with a basic understanding of circuit bending.

Once you've achieved a working knowledge of the basics, it won't take long before your creativity and ingenuity take over. Makerspaces have so many great tools to play with. They thrive on new technological developments, so it's no wonder that they're some of the best places around to learn, share, and play.

Makers learn by doing. It's no surprise that many enjoy taking devices apart, modifying them, and using their parts to make new instruments. One new trend called circuit bending involves randomly modifying the circuits of electronic musical instruments and other electronics to create unexpected sounds and musical patterns. The outcome is often surprising, which is what draws many people to circuit bending.

Other modern technologies that you might get a chance to experiment with include robotics, computer programming, and laser engraving, to name just a few. These areas of interest allow makers to push the boundaries of music as they search for novel techniques, methods, sounds, and styles.

UNDERSTANDING MUSICAL SOFTWARE

Computers have become an integral tool of electronic music. Advances in computer technology result in new ways to create music. In addition to high-tech devices and computers in makerspaces, you can also find cutting-edge software. Depending on the makerspace, you might find software for making, editing, mixing, and recording music. Other examples include tuners, drum machines, metronomes, CD burners, and DJ tools.

Makerspaces thrive on open-source software. "Open-source" means the software's creators allow other people to make changes to the program and even distribute it to others. A lot of open-source software is available for free on the Internet. Open-source software is used for a large number of jobs and projects. Popular open-source music software includes Hydrogen Drum Machine and Csound, a computer programming language for sound.

MUSICAL HARDWARE

Open-source hardware has also helped do-it-yourself musicians achieve new sounds and creations. Most are inexpensive, easy to use, and customizable. The hardware consists of physical components, particularly printed circuit boards. These boards are used to make microcontrollers. Microcontrollers are used to make a vast array of inventions, from remote-controlled robots to mechanical instruments. Another benefit of using open-source hardware includes online resources, including schematics, instructions, forums, and the open-source software needed for numerous purposes.

Arduino, one of the most popular open-source hardware producers out there, is used extensively by hobbyists, scientists, and of course musicians. Arduino kits come with premade microcontroller boards with both input and output connections. Some makers prefer to fabricate printed circuit boards and install the chips, transistors, and connections themselves. Open-source hardware gives musicians and instrument makers far more options to choose from.

MAKING MUSIC WITH ARDUINO

If you've never worked with Arduino microcontrollers, you might be surprised to find how easy and fun they are to use. Makers use Arduino kits for countless projects, including music. Being open-source, Arduino projects are well supported by online details, diagrams, photographs, videos, and forums. A glance online will show you just how enterprising open-source experimenters can be. Arduino fans have used open-source hardware and software to make robotic drum kits, music boxes, stringless guitars, and a lot more. For some of these projects, you can purchase a kit that has everything you need to build your own.

Many instrument makers have used Arduino technology to create their own bizarre instruments, such as an ant farm where ants help make music. The ants' movements are monitored by sensors. The sensors send information through a microprocessor, which converts the movements to sounds. The changing tones create a strange but rhythmic song.

Have you ever seen a laser harp? That may sound impossible, but you can easily find out how to make one with an Arduino microprocessor. A series of laser beams are aimed at photocells. When something, such as a musician's hand, interrupts the laser beam, sensors send information to the Arduino. Then the processor sends information to a computer, which plays different notes. Musicians can even change the quality of the notes by moving their hands around in the beams.

These are just two examples of the amazing instruments people have invented using Arduino technology. They are also exactly the kind of projects you're likely to experience in a makerspace. You may find one to play with, or you might just build one for yourself.

PRINTING IN 3-D

One of the most exciting tools found in makerspaces is the 3-D printer. The process of printing a 3-D object begins with a digital image created on designing software, such as computer-aided design (CAD). The printer reads the design and then produces layer upon layer of rubber, plastic, paper, metal, or another material until a digital design takes shape in three dimensions. This technology is destined to revolutionize many industries, including music and musical instruments.

Pan flutes are one of the simplest instruments to make on a 3-D printer. In fact, they have been a popular choice

3-D printers can print just about any shape or part you can think of in a wide variety of materials.

for many artists working with 3-D printers. Other artists have created more complex wind instruments, such as a fully functioning flute. Other instruments that have been made with 3-D printers include whistles, recorders, violins, and guitars. Not only that, 3-D printers can be used to make replacements for broken parts, such as a violin tuning peg or a conductor's baton.

CHAPTER SIX

THE INFLUENCE OF ELECTRONIC MUSIC

Electronic music is any music that involves the use of electronic equipment to make or modify sounds, which are broadcast through loudspeakers. These instruments can include organs, synthesizers, computers, amplifiers, and microphones. Electronic music has become increasingly popular today, but you might be surprised to hear that it's been popular on and off for close to ninety years.

The earliest electronic instruments came about because of innovations made in electrical components. Oscillating circuits, vacuum tubes, and transistors gave inventors brand-new technology to work with, and some inventors, such as those mentioned in this chapter, wasted little time creating exciting new instruments. Their discoveries have inspired future generations of musicians and inventors to create new musical methods and instruments.

This photograph from around 1970 shows Robert Moog posing with a Moog synthesizer. Today, synthesizers take up much less room!

LOOK, MA! NO HANDS!

In 1920, Russian inventor Leon Theremin invented the first mass-produced electronic instrument—the Theremin. When he was young, Theremin enjoyed experimenting with electricity and different types of oscillations, or swaying motions. A clock pendulum is an example of a mechanical oscillator because it continuously swings back and forth. An electronic oscillator is an electric circuit that produces a repetitive signal. At the time, glass oscillators, or vacuum tubes, were a new innovation. A glass tube with a vacuum inside can be made to conduct electricity, change its direction, and change the form of the electricity. Vacuum tubes have been used for countless purposes, including radios, televisions, computers, and guitar amplifiers.

Theremin had been working on an electric device for measuring the density of gases. However, he realized the device made changing sounds when he held his hands near it. Theremin built a wooden case that housed two vacuum tubes, each connected to an antenna. The antennas generated magnetic fields. A musician plays the Theremin by moving his or her hands around in the magnetic fields. One antenna controls pitch, and the other controls volume. Theremin's no-hands instrument amazed people of the time. Truth is, the Theremin is still an amazing instrument—one that you and your friends can make for yourselves.

LEON THEREMIN:
GRANDFATHER OF ELECTRONIC MUSIC

Even from an early age, Leon Theremin was a true maker. He was interested in both science and math, and he began studying physics before high school. He also played the piano, violin, and cello.

In the years leading up to 1920, inventors in the Soviet Union eagerly experimented with electricity. Theremin saw this as a chance to make a new kind of instrument. When Theremin demonstrated the electronic instrument to people at an electronics show in Moscow, he became an instant celebrity. Even Soviet leader Vladimir Lenin was impressed. Theremin toured the world with his futuristic musical instrument.

Theremin's invention appeared regularly in musical and scientific circles throughout its existence. Because the Theremin creates an eerie sound, it was used to create a creepy atmosphere for horror movies during the 1940s and 1950s. Innovative rock musicians of the 1960s and 1970s, such as Pink Floyd, the Beach Boys, and Led Zeppelin, used the Theremin. Several concert compositions have been written for the Theremin, and they are still performed by Thereminists today.

As a trained cellist, Theremin used electrical technology to make a stringless cello. He also worked with an American inventor to develop the first electric drum machine. Musical historians often credit Leon Theremin with helping to shape the musical landscape of the twentieth century.

Leon Theremin demonstrated in 1927 just how his invention worked.

During an interview in 1989, when asked why he made the electronic instrument, Theremin told his interviewer, "I became interested in effectuating progress in music so that there would be more resources... I was interested in making a different kind of instrument... Therefore I transformed electronic equipment into a musical instrument that would provide greater resources." Theremin's words capture the attitude of modern DIYers and makerspaces. Theremin took new technology of the time and used it to create new instruments. Electronic music might not be the same without his amazing inventions.

HAMMOND AND LESLIE

Another important early electronic instrument is the Hammond organ. Created by American inventor Laurens Hammond in the 1930s, the Hammond organ ran on a silent electrical motor. The motor turned a series of tone wheels, which are metal cogs with even bumps on the rim. Each tone wheel spins near an electronic device called a pickup. It's the same thing that changes the mechanical vibrating strings of an electrical guitar into amplified notes. Hammond's unique instrument was a huge hit, especially with churches.

Another American inventor, Don Leslie, created a speaker that spins, now called the Leslie. When used with an organ, it creates a different type of sound quality. The spinning speakers create a warm, wavering musical effect. In 1954, Hammond released his first Leslie speaker—the B-3—and a musical legend was born. The B-3 was eagerly embraced by jazz, pop, rock, gospel, and soul musicians who helped create the revolutionary music of the 1950 and 1960s.

Hammond and Leslie weren't musicians; they were makers. They recognized how burgeoning technology could be used to make new musical instruments. Many others have followed their leads in music technology, including Robert Moog, the man many consider to be electronic music's most influential pioneer.

SYNTHESIZERS AND MOOG

The synthesizer has been one of the genre's most important instruments for years. It is used to make, or "synthesize," a wide variety of tones, sounds, and effects. Synthesizers can include a keyboard and a range of controls and inputs to connect to other devices. The earliest synthesizers, developed in the 1950s, used mechanical parts. Some produced and read paper tape with holes punched in it.

Growing up in Queens, New York, Robert Moog's mother taught him to play the piano, and his father taught him about electrical engineering. He built his own Theremin when he was just fourteen. He started a mail-order company and sold enough Theremins to pay his way through college. Even after Moog got his Ph.D. in engineering physics, he continued to sell Theremin kits. He used the profit to develop other electronic instruments.

Around 1960, the voltage-controlled oscillator (VCO) was invented. VCOs allowed Moog to remove the mechanical parts from synthesizers, making changes instantaneous. Moog used VCO "modules" to create the first modular analog synthesizer. Each module on the synthesizer manipulates a different sound quality, such as pitch and volume, and can add other features such as fading and tremolo. All these qualities could be adjusted quickly with a set of dials and switches. Moog also used transistors to make smaller synthesizers, which were far more affordable and accessible. They quickly grew widely popular, thanks to musicians of the 1960s, such as the Beach Boys and the Beatles.

Fans of electronic music (as well as other musical styles) often credit Moog with changing the music industry. His synthesizers allowed musicians to experiment with different sounds and effects, and people are still using them today.

INSPIRING THE FUTURE

Today, electronic music is more popular than ever before. Part of its success is because of superstar performers such as Daft Punk, Radiohead, and Gorillaz. Electronic music has a big presence in movie sound tracks, video games, and commercials. Some concert music has been composed for electronic instruments, too.

The Kawasaki Electronic Digital Guitar was sold in the late 1980s. Today, some makers acquire them at garage sales and junk stores to practice circuit bending on them.

Electronic music has also become a popular makerspace concentration, especially with teenagers. In part, electronic music fans have helped make makerspaces successful. Makerspaces give young musicians an opportunity to work with technology they might not otherwise have access to. Tomorrow's top electronic music stars might be learning in makerspaces right now.

46

CHAPTER SEVEN

GETTING EVEN MORE OUT OF MAKERSPACES

As discussed earlier, there are many different opportunities available to musicians who attend makerspaces. There are traditional techniques, high-tech developments, and resources for fans of electronic music. However, there's even more than that. Makerspaces often have meet-ups for audio engineers, musical producers, programmers, and others who are interested in musical endeavors. This chapter will address musical interests and activities that fall just outside many of the topics already addressed.

MAKERSPACES AND COMPUTER PROGRAMMING

Much like electronic music, computer music is a field that you may be able to explore in a makerspace. This includes any computer processes used to create digital sounds. Compared to other forms of music and music production, computer music leans heavily on mathematics in addition to music theory. You might be surprised to hear that there are numerous music programming languages, known as audio programming languages. They are specially designed to develop music production software, much of which is open-source.

With the popularity of mobile technology, programmers have created countless applications for use on smartphones and tablets. Music-themed phone apps are both useful and entertaining. You might make a guitar tuner, a metronome, or an interactive musical toy. If you're interested in both programming and music, designing music-related software is something you can explore in a makerspace.

MUSIC PRODUCTION AND DEEJAYING

Audio engineers are an important part of the recording industry. They work with all kinds of musicians inside recording studios. They record, edit, manipulate, mix, and produce music. Many of your favorite albums sound as good as they do thanks to audio engineers. They may also help produce music for films, animated movies, video games, and live music.

Some makerspaces feature recording studios where you can learn the science and practices behind music production. This includes working with mixing boards and other standard equipment. You may get the chance to help musicians create professional-level music and sound effects. You may also use video recording equipment and green screens in makerspaces. These give musicians the opportunity to create professional music videos and demonstrations.

Some makerspaces have started programs to help train DJs. DJs, short for "disk jockeys," are performers who have traditionally used turntables and records to play music for an audience. In the past, DJs would play music and talk, but the art has transformed into a more creative pastime. Today's DJs play music, mix music, and perform percussive "scratching" on musical equipment. Some are music producers as well.

Aspiring DJs have a lot of cool technology to play with, including turntables, mixing boards, sequencers, synthesizers, MIDI controllers, and a range of effects devices. They use vinyl records, CDs, and computer files to make music. A makerspace sound studio might supply some or all of these tools, or another member might share them.

Musical creativity is fostered in many ways at makerspaces. Often the best way to learn how to perform and produce music is to be surrounded by talented musicians.

"HACKING" MUSIC

Makerspaces allow musicians from diverse backgrounds to meet and discuss musical concepts, traditions, and technological advances. With all this musical and technical knowledge coming together in one place, it's hard not to "hack" existing trends and traditions to produce unique works of art and music. You might have an interest in stringed instruments, while someone else might be into robotics. Imagine what two people could invent by combining their skills and knowledge.

Makerspaces provide the perfect place for musicians to gather and just play together. Some compose music together. Collaboration and experimentation are key to musical growth.

What's MIDI?

Musical instrument digital interface, or MIDI, is an electronic music industry standard that allows electronic instruments, computers, and musical devices to "talk" to each other. Synthesizers with microprocessors appeared in 1978. However, it was difficult and often impossible to find synthesizer brands that were compatible with each other. In 1983, synthesizer manufacturers agreed to adopt universal music software that would allow any electronic instrument to connect to and work with any other electronic instrument.

When you record music using MIDI, music software saves it as a file on a computer. This is not a sound or music file. Rather, it contains a set of instructions for recreating a sound, note, or composition. Many people compare it to sheet music because MIDI data tells an electronic device exactly how to generate music, note for note.

MIDI files created on one synthesizer can be uploaded to other computers and electronic instruments. They can even be played back on cell phones. Synthesizer software reads the file and reproduces the music by following the instructions. Musicians can use editing software to change notes, add notes, slow down the tempo, increase note intensity, and much more.

This technology allows a single musician to control multiple electronic instruments. Synthesizers can be linked together to play the same patterns but in different notes. A single key on a keyboard can be set to start another synthesizer playing a preprogrammed base line. Another key can start up a drum machine. Musicians can even control lights and smoke effects.

MIDI has also revolutionized music production. Software allows musicians to record, create, edit, and manipulate music. Audio engineers use computers to integrate multiple electronic instruments and components. Much like Arduino microprocessors, MIDI technology is free. You'll find plenty of open-source MIDI software, including music editors, sequencers, file converters, samplers, players, and more. You're sure to learn much more about MIDI technology at a makerspace.

CHAPTER EIGHT

GETTING STARTED WITH MAKERSPACES

Finding a makerspace in your area might be difficult depending on where you live. Nowadays, most cities have plenty of makerspace options to choose from. Some are privately owned and funded. Others are part of a national network and receive funding from major corporations. Finding them usually isn't hard because they all stay well connected through the Internet. For people who live farther away from cities, your options probably won't be as good. The makerspaces you are able to get to may not have the technologies you'd like to work with.

As the DIY movement grows stronger and more influential, many schools and universities have found new ways to provide students with hands-on learning environments. The initiatives often start small; sometimes makerspace supplies are placed in tubs and bins and then stored in closets during classes. Others set up makerspaces in tech shops, libraries, unused classrooms, and any other available space. In time, many of these spaces have grown into well-stocked workshops and labs.

School and public libraries have become a leading force in creating the makerspaces of the future. Libraries that have been around for many years are being redesigned to offer the public modern machinery and to foster the DIY spirit. Many are transforming from silent study areas to sophisticated learning centers that cater to inventors, craftspeople, artists, and other makers. Libraries have long been community centers for education, sharing resources, and enjoyment. More than ever before, thanks to makerspaces, libraries are becoming the perfect place to learn, play, invent, share, and have fun.

MAKERSPACES ONLINE

By definition, a makerspace occurs in a physical place. But let's say you can't find a convenient makerspace near your home. The next best thing is to get on the Internet. The Internet might lack in-person interaction, which is a strength of makerspaces. Yet, it is the single most important repository of makerspace "stuff." The list of makerspace projects you can find online is practically limitless. Most include highly detailed and user-friendly plans, designs, diagrams, primers, and much more. Videos can show you how to play music, repair an instrument, and use music-related software. You can order just about any tool or material you might need. You can also use the Internet to seek out makerspaces that are opening up in your area.

MAKER MANNERS

Makerspaces are shared locations. There are a lot of other people to consider when you hang out in one. It's important to follow a makerspace's rules and safety practices, which are in place to protect everyone. Always respect makerspace managers, leaders, and instructors. As mentioned, it can be expensive to operate a makerspace, so be respectful of the tools, supplies, and other resources you find there. While exploration and play are key concepts behind the success of makerspaces, refrain from destructive or distracting behavior.

The people you meet at a makerspace, regardless of their interests and skill levels, are often enthusiastic about meeting and working with new people. You should walk into a makerspace with a positive attitude and an open mind. Arguments over resources, tools, and project space create a negative atmosphere, which is detrimental to a shared community workspace. Prejudiced attitudes won't be tolerated. It's your responsibility to help make the makerspace an enjoyable place for everyone.

Just because you are a member of a makerspace doesn't make it your duty to help others. However, by passing on the chance to share what you know with less experienced people, you're really not getting the most out of the maker movement. Teaching reinforces knowledge. It can also be gratifying to help others learn something that you've learned, perhaps from someone in the same makerspace. This continuing peer-to-peer interaction might be the makerspace's greatest benefit of all.

Perhaps most important, the Internet offers DIY blogs, podcasts, and forums, which allow many kinds of people to interact and share knowledge, just as physical makerspaces do. It may not be the same as meeting people face to face, but

At a recent Maker Carnival in Beijing, China, spectators listened to a mechanical glass harp.

then again, video conferencing has brought the whole world closer together. Makers on the opposite ends of the world can meet at any time.

DO IT YOURSELF

Despite all the great advice in this resource, you may not have many makerspaces where you live. The ones you do find might not focus on music or musical instruments. In this case, you might think about leading a charge to establish one in your community.

It can be hard to fund a makerspace because it requires a considerable amount of startup money. Try speaking to local parents, teens, teachers, and leaders to see what the possibilities are. Chances are you will find others who support your ambitions. Makerspaces require a constant supply of funds to keep them running. Fortunately, there are organizations that donate money, fund projects, and offer grants to people who set up makerspaces.

A music makerspace is the perfect place to start when you're interested in making your own musical instruments. Most musicians understand the benefit of playing with and learning from others, especially in a relaxed forum outside the classroom. It also makes learning more fun.

amplifier An electrical device that makes sounds louder.

computer-aided design (CAD) Precision drawing software used by artists, architects, and engineers.

electronic oscillator A circuit that produces a repetitive signal and changes direct current to alternating current.

genre A category of art, writing, or music.

hacker Originally, a computer programmer. Today, it is more often associated with someone able to break into computer systems.

hybrid Involving mixed parts.

magnetic field The region around a magnet or moving electrical charge where the force of magnetism functions.

medium The materials and processes used by an artist or musician.

microcontroller A small computer contained on a single microchip (or integrated circuit).

MIDI controller Hardware or software that allows different devices to exchange musical information.

module Independent parts that can be put together to make a more complex device.

photocell A device that uses light to create electricity.

primer An introduction to a given topic, usually in writing.

PVC Polyvinyl chloride; a common, durable plastic.

salvage To remove something from the garbage and repair or use it.

sequencer An electronic device the stores and replays sequences of musical notes.

voltage Electrical potential expressed in volts, a unit of energy."

International Computer Music Association
1819 Polk Street, Suite 330
San Francisco, CA 94109
Website: http://www.computermusic.org
This association is a group of people and institutions that are involved in all aspects of computer music.

The Make House
833 1/2 Fort Street
Victoria, BC V8W 1H6
Canada
Website: http://www.themakehouse.ca
(778) 432-2294
This makerspace in Victoria, Canada, features numerous classes and workshops, as well as special projects for children.

Maker Media
1005 Gravenstein Highway North
Sebastopol, CA 95472
Website: http://www.makermedia.com
Publisher of *Make magazine* and a library of DIY guides, Maker Media is one of the biggest promoters of the maker-space movement.

National Endowment for the Arts (NEA)
1100 Pennsylvania Avenue NW
Washington, DC 20506
Website: http://www.arts.gov
(202) 682-5400

An agency of the U.S. federal government, the NEA supports and funds art projects exhibiting artistic excellence.

New York Hall of Science
47-01 111th Street
Corona, NY 11368
Website: http://makerspace.nysci.org
This is a hands-on museum dedicated to science, technology, engineering, and math. It features science clubs, camps, and a popular makerspace program for kids.

ThingTank Lab
DDiMIT Consortium
376 Bathurst
Toronto, ON M5T 2S6
Canada
Website: http://www.thingtanklab.com
ThingTank Lab is a Canadian group that refers to itself as "an open, community based collaborative ideation lab." Includes links to other Canadian makerspaces.

WEBSITES

Due to the changing nature of Internet links, Rosen Publishing has developed an online list of websites related to the subject of this book. This site is updated regularly. Please use this link to access the list:

http://www.rosenlinks.com/MAKER/Instr

Baichtal, John. *Hack This: 24 Incredible Hackerspace Projects from the DIY Movement.* Indianapolis, IN: Que, 2012.

Cline, Dallas. *How to Play Nearly Everything from Bones and Spoons to the Washtub Bass.* New York, NY: Oak Publications, 1977.

Deane-Pratt, Ade. *Musical Instruments.* New York, NY: PowerKids Press, 2012.

Gifford, Clive. *Cool Tech: Gadgets, Games Robots, and the Digital World.* New York, NY: DK Publishing, 2011.

Helsby, Genevieve. *Those Amazing Musical Instruments!* Naperville, IL: Sourcebooks, 2007.

Kemp, Adam. *The Makerspace Workbench.* Sebastopol, CA: Maker Media, 2013.

Miles, Liz. *Playing the Spoons and Other Curious Instruments.* Chicago, IL: Raintree, 2011.

O'Neill, Terence. *Arduino.* Ann Arbor, MI: Cherry Lake Publishing, 2014.

Roslund, Samantha. *Maker Faire.* Ann Arbor, MI: Cherry Lake Publishing, 2014.

Roslund, Samantha. *Makerspaces.* Ann Arbor, MI: Cherry Lake Publishing, 2014.

Tomecek, Stephen M. *Music.* New York, NY: Chelsea House, 2010.

VanHecke, Susan. *Raggin' Jazzin' Rockin': A History of American Musical Instrument Makers.* Honesdale, PA: Boyds Mills Press, 2011.

Wilson, Ray. Make: *Analog Synthesizers.* Sebastopol, CA: Maker Media, 2013.

American Libraries. "Manufacturing Makerspaces." February 6, 2013. Retrieved December 2, 2013 (http://www .americanlibrariesmagazine.org/article/manufacturing -makerspaces).

Baichtal, John. *Hack This: 24 Incredible Hackerspace Projects from the DIY Movement.* Indianapolis, IN: Que, 2012.

Biography.com. "Robert Arthur Moog." The Biography Channel Website, 2013. Retrieved December 3, 2013 (http://www.biography.com/people/robert-moog -21338711).

Britton, Lauren. "The Makings of Maker Spaces." The Digital Shift, October 1 2012. Retrieved December 3, 2013 (http://www.thedigitalshift.com/2012/10/public -services/the-makings-of-maker-spaces-part-1 -space-for-creation-not-just-consumption).

HammondOrgan.com. "Hammond/Leslie Heritage." Retrieved December 3, 2013 (http://hammondorganco. com/about-us/company-profile).

Hiller, Lejaren. "Electronic Music." Encyclopaedia Britannica Online. Retrieved December 4, 2013 (http:// www.britannica.com/EBchecked/topic/183823/ electronic-music).

Kemp, Adam. *The Makerspace Workbench.* Sebastopol, CA: Maker Media, 2013.

Makerspace.com staff. *High School Makerspace Tools and Materials.* March 14, 2012. Retrieved December 2, 2013 (http://makerspace.com/wp-content/uploads/ 2012/03/makerspace-hs-toolsmaterials.pdf).

Makerspace.com staff. *Makerspace Playbook*, Spring 2013. Retrieved December 2, 2013 (http://makerspace.com/wp-content/uploads/2013/02/MakerspacePlaybook -Feb2013.pdf).

Malinka, Kali. "Jug Bands: The DIY Movement in Music." *Concordia Undergraduate Journal of Art History*. Retrieved December 3, 2013 (http://cujah.org/essay -7-volume-vii).

MIDI Manufacturers Association. "History of MIDI." Retrieved December 9, 2013 (http://www.midi.org/aboutmidi/tut_history.php).

Mings, Josh. "RimbaTubes: The PVC Pipe Instrument That Will Slap Your Ears in the Face." Solidsmack, May 28, 2013. Retrieved December 3, 2013 (http://solidsmack .com/design/rimbatubes-the-pvc-pipe-instrument-that -will-slap-your-ears-in-the-face).

OddMusic.com. "The Theremin." Retrieved December 4, 2013 (http://www.oddmusic.com/theremin/index.html).

Roos, Dave. "How MIDI Works." HowStuffWorks.com, March 18, 2008. Retrieved December 9, 2013 (http://entertainment.howstuffworks.com/midi.htm).

Team Hugh Manatee. "What Are Makerspaces?" Retrieved December 2, 2013 (http://teamhughmanatee.wordpress .com/about).

Vennard, Martin. "Leon Theremin: The Man and the Music Machine." BBC News, March 12, 2012. Retrieved December 2, 2013 (http://www.bbc.co.uk/news/magazine-17340257).

ABOUT THE AUTHOR

Greg Roza has been writing books and educational materials for fifteen years. He lives in Hamburg, New York, with his wife and three children. Roza is an amateur musician who plays the trombone and bass guitar. He also enjoys tinkering with machinery in his spare time.

PHOTO CREDITS

Designer: Nelson Sá; Editor: Nicholas Croce;
Photo Researcher: Amy Feinberg